The Magic Clog Dancer

Written by
Cath Jones

Illustrated by
Andy Hamilton

The king was hopping mad.

There were rabbits on the loose in the castle garden!

Munch! Crunch!

Those rabbits ate up everything.

"Who can catch those rabbits?" asked the king. "I will bake a colossal rabbit pie!"

Traps were set, but those rabbits were clever and quick.

They slid down the castle chimneys and merrily ate all the food in the kitchen!

No one could capture the rabbits!

The king did not have a clue what he should do.

"Offer a reward," said the queen.

"I will hand out gold to the person who can capture the rabbits!" called the king.

Up stepped Mrs Dancer!
"*I* will capture those rabbits," she said.

At dawn, Mrs Dancer crept out of bed.

She put on her magic wooden clogs and began tap dancing!

"Listen!" said the king.

Clack-clackity-clack went the clogs.

Whenever she went clack-clackity-clack, the rabbits began dancing too!

They could not resist.

When Mrs Dancer went clack-clackity-clack into the castle and down into the kitchen, so did the rabbits!

Those rabbits hopped directly into the king's colossal pie dish!

By the afternoon, not one rabbit was left in the castle garden.

"Can I collect my reward of gold now?" Mrs Dancer asked.

But the king was too mean to pay!

"All that clacking has given me a headache," he said.

So Mrs Dancer put on her magic clogs again …

… clack-clackity-clack.

The clack-clackity-clacking woke up the rabbits. Suddenly the king began dancing!

The rabbits hopped out of the pie and ...

... the king hopped in!